Come Alive Now

Come Alive Now

Step Into a Full
and Free Life

Leah Fruth

*To my husband, Trevor, who always knew that this
dream was possible and reminded me of it when I
so often forgot.*

*To my kids, Jasper, Ellis, and Crosby.
I stepped into this healing process for you.
You were the reason I wanted to come back to life,
and for that, this book is for you too.*

Contents

Author's Note

This book can be done on its own, but to get the full experience, go to www.leahfruth.com/comealivenow to sign up for the seven week course.

The course is taught by me, Leah Fruth, and comes with instruction, weekly teaching videos and workout videos, along with additional printables.

Foreword

It was the beginning of 2020, a new year with much unknown ahead. Little did I know that the pandemic would hit a few months into the start of this new year. God was working, as always, and brought my dear friend, Leah, into my life. I know many of us can get tired and weary from social media, but I will also say that it is a place to grow, connect and share our lives with one another. This is where God crossed our paths and our friendship began.

I will never forget one of our first conversations on grief and suffering that we had and the words Leah spoke over me were, "wander deeper in". As we shared all the different parts of our journeys through suffering, there was always an overwhelming truth that lingered between us – the journey through pain and suffering is a beautiful place where grief and His goodness collide.

Fast forward and getting to walk and pray alongside Leah and all that God has been working in and through her has been a blessing to my life. I wholeheartedly believe that you too will feel this as you read and journey through Come Alive Now. This book is an anthem of Leah's heart as she helps us to really fix our eyes on our mighty God in the circumstances we are navigating in the everyday moments of our lives.

As I stand at the threshold of Leah's transformative journey that is held within these pages, I am struck by the profound truth embedded in her words, "surrender the outcome to Him." This simple yet profound principle serves as the cornerstone upon which Leah's story unfolds, and indeed, it beckons us all into the depths of our own encounters with the Lord.

In the tumultuous currents of life, where loss, pain, grief, and trauma threaten to engulf us, Leah's journey stands as a testament to the redemptive power of God's love and grace. Within these chapters, she generously invites us into the sacred spaces of her own healing process—a journey marked by surrender, obedience, and an unwavering faith in the goodness of God.

As Leah walked through her years of healing, she spurred me on in my healing. Each conversation and the words she wrote for myself and others to read were not just mending, but a profound sense, a revival in her bones that breathed new life over her life and those around her. It was a journey that led her from the shadows of despair into the radiant light of God's presence—a journey from brokenness to wholeness, from captivity to freedom. The beautiful thing about it all was that through her sharing God's character, grace, mercy, and work, she showed me that the further I wander into the grief with Him, healing would be possible. I find myself in this ongoing healing process everyday as the hills and valleys ebb and flow as I walk through being a mother of a child with disabilities. Yet, one thing stands out through getting to be a witness to Leah living out the message of Come Alive Now, is hope.

As Leah's words flow across the pages, it becomes abundantly clear that her heart beats with a singular passion—to see us set free, chains shattered, and lives transformed by the power of Christ's love. With each word, she extends a hand of solidarity to those who journey alongside her—a companion in the wilderness, a beacon of hope amidst the darkness.

This book is not merely a collection of insights or a roadmap to healing; it is an invitation—a call to come alive, to embark on the journey of healing and restoration that is possible for you and for me with God. It is a testament to the resilience that God has equipped us with and the boundless depths of God's unfailing love.

Leah's fervor, her unwavering commitment to see others set free, reverberates through every syllable, every sentence. She is more than an author; she is a steadfast ally, a faithful guide, journeying alongside each reader as they navigate the terrain of their own healing process.

I have no doubt that you will be emboldened by Leah's courage, inspired by her unwavering faith, and captivated by the transformative power of God's love. May these pages serve as a safe space—a sacred space where wounds are healed, hearts are restored, a place where you will meet God, and truly see His goodness in the midst of it all.

Leah invites you to come alive, now. Wander deeper in.

His ways forward,
Jennifer Edewaard

Hi Friends,

That's me at age nine in that picture. It is the year before my life was altered by pain and loss. At nine, I knew what I loved and loved who I was fully. I bet you can remember a before; a time when you were fully yourself and fully alive. That is the person we are going to get back to in this time together. I am incredibly grateful that I get to walk alongside you in this process. I do not take it lightly that you have chosen to trust me with your time.

Right now, I want you to sit back.
Relax.
Lower your shoulders, and take a deep breath.

Welcome. I call you friends because that is what you are now. I come to you not only to share Jesus with you, but to share my life with you as well.

1 Thessalonians 2:8 says, "We cared so much for you that we were pleased to share with you not only the gospel of God but also our own lives, because you had become dear to us."

You are dear to me, and I want you to know that I'm not going to hold back from you. I'm asking you not to hold back either. Make the choice now to be all in; all in on sharing your life with me and the people around you in this process. But mostly, all in on allowing God to do what He wants to do in this time. This is your first action step: surrender the outcome to Him.

The story that has been written over my life is God's story. He has used EVERYTHING in my life to point back to Him and His glory. God has taken my story of loss, pain, grief, trauma, and unhealth and redeemed it into a story of encountering the love of God and the freedom of Jesus. He has led me to the full life that only He gives. He has brought me back to life.

Before we get into this any further, here is the abbreviated version of my story. I have experienced great loss in my life. I grew up the oldest of three children, with two loving parents. My Dad was very sick for years, in and out of the hospital, and died when I was ten. My mom remarried, we moved, and they added four more boys to our family throughout my middle school years.

From my perspective, even though I wouldn't have been able to put words to it at the time, I had lost not only my Dad, but my home, my school, my friends, the closeness to my grandparents, and the family that I had once had. Everything was different in a short amount of time, and I didn't know where I fit.

Those years were rough. Looking back, I was dealing with a lot of trauma on my own, and it was having its effect on me. I thought it was just my nature, but the traumas and stresses continuing to be stuffed were building up into anxiety. (Side note: None of us were made with anxiety. If you think it is just the way you are, like I did, it is not.)

Fast forward to adulthood…I married my high school sweetheart, moved back to our hometown, and grew closer to my mom and siblings than ever before. I still had not dealt with any of my own pain, but life was good enough to ignore it all. Then, when my first child was nine months old, we found out that my mom had pancreatic cancer. My world crumbled in an instant.

I poured everything I had into being with her, taking care of her and my siblings, taking care of my own new family, and also running my photography business at the time. I believed that I had no time to think about my own pain. At least that is what I told myself. I think I believed that if I was able to keep doing for everyone else, I must be doing good enough.

The years after my mom's death, I continued to take care of my siblings while we added children to our own growing family. I fell deeper and deeper into anxiety without ever knowing that that was what it was. I just knew I was struggling. It took my youngest twin brothers graduating, and all of a sudden losing the distraction of always making sure they were ok, to realize that I wasn't. It was time to get help myself.

This book is what came out of three years of doing the work to heal, surrendering it to God, being obedient to His voice, and letting Him love me! It took three years for Him to heal me and set me free, but it is three years that I would not change. I grew closer to God, and He taught me so much.

Now, I want to give that to you. But know this…it most likely will be a process that you will continue past these six weeks. These practices that you will learn will be something that, hopefully, will become a part of your life. They are how I still fight against the darkness and walk in the light. Trust what God has in store for you. He is faithful.

There aren't many rules on how you go through this book, but I do have a few. Here are the ground rules:

01

Begin by welcoming God into this process with you.

Nothing is going to change in you if you are hoping this workshop is going to be the magic pill that is going to help you or heal you. You are not going to be able to work hard enough or perfect enough to make this work. ONLY GOD can do the deep work in you.

Begin with a prayer. Maybe one that goes something like this. Feel free to repeat this prayer. Use your voice out loud. There is power in speaking it.

God, You truly are my loving Father. Your love for me is so great, and I know that your ways for my life are the best ways because only you can see the whole picture. I surrender the time of this workshop to you. I trust you to do the work in me that only you can do. Give me the discipline to keep showing up throughout these weeks, to do the hard work, and to choose you over everything else. Keep my focus on you, and you alone. Thank you for breathing life into me, and bringing me back to who you always created me to be! Amen

02

Be willing to do the work.

I know I just said that only God can do the deep work inside of you, which is true, but you also have to show up. If you only read the material and do not actively participate in any of the activities, not much will probably change. Make the promise to yourself now that you are going to show up each week and do the work.

03 Don't quit!

When it gets hard, and it will at some point, promise yourself that you will not quit. If you have a bad week, miss some of the activities, DON'T QUIT! Jump back in. Keep showing up. It will be worth it.

04 No comparing your life circumstances to anyone else's.

If you are doing this in a group, I hope that you are able to build and strengthen relationships within your group. If you are going through this alone, this rule still applies to you. You are not going to compare your circumstances or life experiences to others'. Not to mine or anyone else around you, nor to anyone online. You aren't going to say things like, "Wow, she has gone through so much and has had so many struggles. My struggles aren't close to as bad as hers so why can't I get it together?", or "My pain is minimal compared to hers so it is not even worth acknowledging."

We simply cannot compare life circumstances and struggles. I want you to care for others, but do not let it deter you from your own work.

05 Find a prayer partner.

It is a huge encouragement when we know someone is lifting us up in prayer. If you are going through Come Alive Now in a group, assign prayer partners to each other. Pray for one another throughout the duration of your time together. If you are going through this as an individual, tell one person that you are going through this book and ask them to be praying for you throughout. Be vulnerable and willing to ask for prayer as you need it.

Set a schedule for yourself.

When we do not plan, we often struggle to follow through with any good intentions. Ask yourself these questions: When will be the start of each week for me? What day will I read the material? When will I work on the homework? If you are taking the online course, when will you do the workout and watch the teaching videos?

Create a schedule for yourself. This is a good starting point, but remember, if you get off track, don't quit!

Sign up for the online course.

This book can be done on its own, but to get the full experience, go to www.leahfruth.com/comealivenow to sign up for the 7 Week Course.

The Course includes weekly videos from Leah with additional teaching, workout videos, and additional printables.

Are you ready to get started?
Are you ready to Come Alive Now?

**Before we begin, we are going to do one thing. Let's read Ezekiel 37:1-10.
Let these words fill your mind and heart.**

The hand of the Lord was on me, and he brought me out by his Spirit and set me down in the middle of the valley; it was full of bones. He led me all around them. There were a great many of them on the surface of the valley, and they were very dry. Then he said to me, "Son of man, can these bones live?"

I replied, "Lord God, only you know."

He said to me, "Prophesy concerning these bones and say to them: Dry bones, hear the word of the Lord! This is what the Lord God says to these bones: I will cause breath to enter you, and you will live. I will put tendons on you, make flesh grow on you, and cover you with skin. I will put breath in you so that you come to life. Then you will know that I am the Lord."

So I prophesied as I had been commanded. While I was prophesying, there was a noise, a rattling sound, and the bones came together, bone to bone. As I looked, tendons appeared on them, flesh grew, and skin covered them, but there was no breath in them. He said to me, "Prophesy to the breath, prophesy, son of man. Say to it: This is what the Lord God says: Breath, come from the four winds and breathe into these slain so that they may live!" So I prophesied as he commanded me; the breath entered them, and they came to life and stood on their feet, a vast army.

1

There Was Once Life in You

"The hand of the LORD was on me, and he brought me out by his Spirit and set me down in the middle of the valley; it was full of bones. He led me all around them. There were a great many of them on the surface of the valley, and they were very dry."
Ezekiel 37:1-2

I can't begin to know where you are at right now, but I'm wondering if you feel pretty dry. Maybe life isn't at all what you had planned and you're wondering where it all went wrong. Maybe life is exactly what you planned, and yet it feels nothing like you had expected. Maybe the world and everything that felt steady at one time now feels a bit out of control.

I'll never forget a moment I had about four years ago now. It was a slow summer day. At the time my kids were 6, 3, and 6 Months old, and we were sitting in our driveway drawing with sidewalk chalk. Everything around me was perfect. We had recently moved to a house on the street I had always dreamed of living on in my small town. I had three healthy, amazing kids, a loving husband, and the photography business I had always wanted. Yet, I sat there on the driveway and felt nothing. I felt dead inside. I remember thinking that I couldn't even focus my eyes on my kids. I tried to look at them. I tried to enjoy the moment with them. It felt as if I couldn't be present no matter how hard I willed myself to because my mind was on overdrive constantly.

I remember telling myself, "This is just how God made me. A planner, an overthinker, a busy person, a perfectionist...the type A person."

**Genesis 1:27 says, "So God created man in his own image;
he created him in the image of God; he created them male and female."**

When I look to the character of God, nowhere do I find Him described as an overthinker, perfectionist, non-stop busy body. So if I have been made in his image, I was not created this way either. Without any active participation in my healing, my hard life experiences and traumas turned the way I was created as a deep thinker and organized leader into an over thinker, busy body, perfectionist.

This week we are going to look at **Ezekiel 37:1-2.**
"The hand of the LORD was on me, and he brought me out by his Spirit and set me down in the middle of the valley; it was full of bones. He led me all around them. There were a great many of them on the surface of the valley, and they were very dry."

He looked around and the bones were very dry. To be dry means that all wetness or moisture was lost over a period of time. To be dry means that there was once life.

THERE WAS ONCE LIFE! This is what I want you to see this week. I am sure you can look to all the dry areas in your life or how your entire life may feel dry, but that just means, THERE ONCE WAS LIFE in those places. **There once was life IN YOU!**

When we feel dry, we also need to make sure we recognize that sin is what often affects us and pulls life out of us. The sin of the world around us, along with our own sin. We must know and see that we are all sinners in need of a Savior.

When I feel dry and weary, I often come to the realization that my focus has been off. I am able to easily claim that God is most important in my life, but my thoughts and actions say otherwise. Any time anything in our life becomes more important than God, it is idolatry.

Timothy Keller says, "Idolatry means turning a good thing into an ultimate thing." [1]

Alisa Keeton says, "Idols offer you comfort when what you need is courage, feed your fears instead of your faith, and steal your joy for life through a slow and steady spiritual sedation." [2]

What in your life has become an idol? It may be draining you of the courage, faith, and joy that only God can provide. None of this work that we are about to do can be done on our own. We get a choice. We can either white knuckle our way through this, trying to breathe life back into ourselves by making it all about the disciplines, or we can choose to surrender it all to God, making the goal simply to love Him more knowing that He will be the one to breathe life into us throughout our days.

> **John 10:10 says, "The thief comes only to steal and kill and destroy;**
> **I have come that they may have life, and have it to the full." (NIV)**

Sin steals and kills and destroys. Jesus came and died so that we may have life here spiritually and life eternal more abundant and full than we can imagine. We are going to keep our mind on the eternal life He promises to us as believers, while also noticing that He is speaking into our life here also. When we keep our eyes on Jesus, keep God first in our lives, seek Him fervently, and begin to sit in His love, life will become more abundant than we can imagine.

God created us for this abundant life. How did God create you in his image? Where has the world and sin stripped that away? Where have you dried up? We are going to begin to answer these questions.

Last year, I went to a workshop that an author was holding at her house. A lot of the time was focused on journaling and looking back over our life to see what giftings God had put inside of us that we were not living out. The journal prompt that most struck me was this…

We all have a memory, at around the age of 8-10 years old, when something happened where we lost the innocence of believing that everything about ourselves was awesome. This could also be where we recognized sin in us or the people around us and our need for a Savoir whether we knew Him at the time or not. It could have been something as simple as a comment from a peer to as big as a traumatic life event. Who were you at the age right before this event?

For me, I needed to look back to age seven. I began to list out things that I liked to do at that age. If I'm honest, it took me longer than most around me to start writing. It was hard for me to remember what I was like before my Dad got sick, when I realized that my life wasn't the safe, secure place I trusted it to be.

As I finally began to scribble out what I loved to do at age seven, something began to surface. I loved to be active with my body. I loved gymnastics, riding bike, and running around the yard. I loved playing basketball before coaches told me I was no good at it. I loved to be outside simply to be outside before I believed that it was a waste of time to simply sit in the breeze. I loved to be the announcer, microphone and all, as my sister and I put on pretend beauty pageants before I felt self conscious of fully being myself and using my voice.

These were passions and giftings that God put in me from the beginning, from the moment I was created. Yet, I had found reasons to let them go. To think of them as frivolous or a waste of time. To think of myself as not good enough to use them. And in turn, I dried up - my soul, my passions, and my giftings.

This is where we are going to focus on our first homework assignment. You were once fully alive, fully yourself. You felt free to be exactly who God created you to be, in His image. It's time to figure out who that is.

This week, we are going to ask ourselves some questions. We are going to look back, and we are going to look inwardly at our present emotions. We also are going to notice our pain because pain points us to what needs healing.

We are not looking inwardly to know ourselves better. We are looking inwardly so that we can get honest with ourselves and with God.

This work you are going to be doing is not easy, and it will also take your time. So right now, I want you to ask yourself if there are some boundaries that you can put in place so that you will be able to do the work, whether it is a boundary on your time or a boundary that helps you care for yourself as you go through different emotions.

- Do you need to stay away from some apps on your phone? Or delete them all together? In the midst of my healing journey, I had to delete the app, TimeHop. Each morning, I opened it simply thinking that I was seeing past cute pictures of my kids, but it was bringing up every emotion that I had at the time that the photo was taken. Most were taken while I was grieving the sickness or loss of my mom.

- Can you put boundaries in place so that you are sure to get enough sleep? Most adults need 7-8 hours a night. If you are a parent, the age of your kids greatly changes how much sleep you are getting, but can you go to bed instead of watching that Netflix show? Sleep does wonders. It will help you see clearly during this time and help with the range of emotions you may be feeling. Anytime my daughter begins to cry in the late evening we look at each other and say, "It's time to go to bed." Tears, worry, fear and other emotions at night are usually a sign that I simply need to put myself to bed and start a new, fresh day in the morning.

- Are there any people that you need to set boundaries to how much you are around them in this time? People in real life or people that you simply follow on instagram? This is a hard one, but if there is a person that triggers past hurts, it is hard to be around them while you are trying to heal from it. Or if there is a person you follow on Instagram that instantly causes you to feel less than, jealousy, or bitterness, YOU CAN UNFOLLOW. It is completely ok. You can also unfollow people who are going through a health scare or have a child who is sick or has been injured. If it causes you fear over your own family or thinking of every worst case scenario, it is not insensitive for you to unfollow. It is not healthy for us to carry so many people's burdens; we were never meant to carry so much. Write down their names to pray for them, but you do not have to follow every update. When you are in a healthier spot, you may be able to go back to the account.

Are you ready? Are you ready to COME ALIVE? You may be dry now, but I want you to choose to believe right now that God can breathe life back into you!

As I said earlier, we were made in the image of God, but without knowing who God is, it is hard to know who we were made to be. Here is a good resource to know God better. Take some time this week to read through them slowly. (https://tinyurl.com/jzbenbuw)

When I go out looking for self-discovery, I quickly lose my way, but when I go out looking to discover God, I finally know myself.

Homework : Week 1

We are going to ask ourselves daily questions this week. Each morning and evening, take 5 minutes to answer these questions in a journal.

Morning Questions :

1. What does God have for me today? Name the top three things God is asking you to do today. Keep it to three.
2. What is one thing that you are dreading today?
3. How can you reframe the way you are thinking about this?

Throughout the Day :

Be aware of your emotions.
Feel free to write them down when they come. I want you to specifically notice any anger that you feel. Anger is not a primary emotion, but typically comes because you have felt fear or sadness. When you feel angry, take the time to ask why? Have you been hurt in some way? Sad? Fearful? Worried?

Another feeling to be aware of is bitterness. Bitterness can seep in so slowly, and I have found that it grows quickly. Bitterness often shows areas of unforgiveness.

Recognize the feelings and why, and write it down. Noticing your pain points will direct you to what needs to be healed.

Evening Questions :

1. First, look back at your 3 things you were going to focus on today.
2. What did you do well?
3. What could you have done differently?
4. Look back on the thing that you were dreading. How did it go?

These questions are to work on as you have time. Make sure to set aside time early in the week so that you have time to reflect on your response.

It's time to look back to who you were created to be. Think back to a moment in time between the ages of 8-10 when something happened to change the way you looked at the world and yourself. It may take awhile to remember this, and if it does, it's ok. Sit, pray, and listen.

Once you are able to think of this period of time, look back at the age right before this. Ask yourself these questions about yourself at that age, and write them in your journal.

1. What did you love to do? Write them all down, even if it seems small and silly. Scribble it all out.
2. How did it feel to do these things?
3. Circle any of the things that you still find joy in, even if you no longer make time for it.

Another area to think on and pray about this week is what you may need to turn over or surrender to God for these 6 weeks. So often we are filling our lives with things that replace God, that push Him to the outer corners of our life. This is the idolatry that we talked about earlier. When we are constantly filling ourselves and our lives with these things, it is tough to make space for God, to make space for Him to work in our lives. Sit down and get honest with yourself and with God.

- What have you been turning into an idol? What do you need to surrender? Listen to God's gentle nudging. Is it shopping, house projects, cleaning, alcohol, food, social media, work, Netflix, or something else?
- Now the hard part is being obedient to this. Every step of obedience I have taken, God shows up in bigger ways in my life. Now is the time for you to take the next step of obedience. Write out what surrendering this idol will actually look like.

Trust That God Will Breathe Life Back Into You

"Then he said to me, 'Son of man, can these bones live?' I replied, 'Lord, God, only you know.'"
Ezekiel 37:3

After last week, you might feel that by simply making a few changes, you are feeling better. Or maybe, after taking inventory of your emotions and pains, you feel worse thinking there is no way you will ever get out of this pit.

No matter how you are feeling, it is hard to trust God fully. If you are feeling good, it is easy to take control thinking that you can make it better all on your own. It feels easier this way because we get to determine the time table on our healing and how the healing happens. But believe me when I say, any healing that you can control will not be nearly as good as a healing that only God can control.

If you are feeling worse, if the pain seems too much, if you see no way out...it is hard to trust that God can heal you. You may think there is no way, or at least no time soon, so you give up. Trust that God's love for you is so great, more than you could ever imagine, and that He wants this healing for you.

This is my prayer for you all.
"I pray that out of his glorious riches he may strengthen you with power through his Spirit in your inner being, so that Christ may dwell in your hearts through faith. And I pray that you, being rooted and established in love, may have power, together with all the Lord's holy people, to grasp how wide and long and high and deep is the love of Christ, and to know this love that surpasses knowledge—that you may be filled to the measure of all the fullness of God.

Now to him who is able to do immeasurably more than all we ask or imagine, according to his power that is at work within us, to him be glory in the church and in Christ Jesus throughout all generations, for ever and ever! Amen." Ephesians 3:16-21 (NIV)

Read again back through Ezekiel 37:1-10. Don't go on until you read it through.

**Verse 3 says, "Then he said to me, 'Son of man, can these bones live?'
I replied, 'Lord, God, only you know.'"**

Ezekiel had no hope in the bones, but he did have hope in God. He trusted that God knew and knew better than he did. You also don't hear him doubting that God can do it.

Do you trust God in this? Are you trusting that God can truly restore you, breathe life into you, free you, and transform you? Do you believe that He can do this for you? Do you believe that He wants to do this for you?

If you got honest and answered no to some of these questions, we are going to explore this more in a bit.

Here is an example from my own life. A few years ago, right before this journey of healing, my body was screaming at me. My trauma, emotional pain, and anxiety had turned into physical pain. Our bodies truly keep the score even when we think we have it all under control. Our bodies tell the truth.

I have watched all 82 seasons of Grey's Anatomy (at least it feels like 82 seasons), and I often write down quotes that stand out to me. This quote feels fitting here from Meredith Grey.

"The human body is a terrible liar. Whatever secrets it's keeping, it will tell them all eventually."
Meredith Grey - Grey's Anatomy [1]

It's true. No matter how much we lie to ourselves that we are ok, that we have things under control, our bodies will begin to tell us when it has become too much.

My body had hit it's limit. I spent three months with severe stomach pain. Every time I ate it would get worse. I did everything in my control to fix it. First, I tried to look at what I was eating, thinking it was a food sensitivity. I got to the point of not eating much of anything, and I was still in pain. I tried some kind of cleanse that a friend swore would help, and my stomach still hurt. I tried gut health drinks and pills that made big promises and cost big money, and my stomach still hurt.

Each time I tried something new, I put all of my hope into it. This was going to be THE THING that fixed it all! My hope was misplaced. My hope was in the product and in myself because I had done the research to find the new product. The only hope I had placed in God was for him to do a miraculous overnight healing. I believed He could do it. I prayed for Him to do it, but if He wasn't going to, I was going to find the next best quick fix.

The stomach pain got to the point where I had to see a doctor. Test after test showed nothing wrong. I was perfectly healthy. The last step was to go to a surgeon that recommended a stomach scope and a colonoscopy, but as he was asking questions and willing to schedule the next tests, he kept repeating one question. "What happened in the Spring when this all started?"

I didn't know how to answer him. Truly, I had no idea, but he kept asking. I scheduled the tests, walked out of the office, got in my car, and on my way home it hit me. That Spring, my youngest brothers had graduated from High School. Since the moment my mom was diagnosed and after she died, I poured all of my energy into taking care of them and trying to make everything hurt less for them, but not for myself. Now that they were out of school and adults, it left a gaping hole. It left me with space to all of a sudden feel my own pain, and in that, my body came crashing down.

This drive home from the surgeon's office was the moment I decided to call a counselor's office. I called the very next day, and I also called and canceled the scope and colonoscopy. This is where

I had to begin trusting God in a process of healing and not the overnight healing that I was desperate for. This is when I realized He was asking me to trust Him to give only one step at a time towards healing.

I needed to be obedient to each step without seeing when or where the healing was going to come. I needed to be obedient even when it was painful, hard, and when it would be easier to try another quick fix.

Here's the thing. We need to trust in God with both the instant healing we know that He is capable of and also in the healing process that may be a long journey.

Do you trust Him? Or are you taking it into your own hands? Only God can do the deep healing that will last. Only the Holy Spirit can heal at the root. Instead of treating the symptoms, let's let God heal at the source of the pain.

Only God can bring life into these dry bones. Ezekiel knew that if anyone could bring the dry bones back to life, it would ONLY be God.

Do you believe that He can and will do this for you? God promises us life and life to the full.

> **John 10:10 says, "The thief comes only to steal and kill and destroy; I (Jesus) have come that they may have life, and have it to the full." (NIV)**

Another version uses the word "abundance" instead of "full". [2] The world has stolen and destroyed so much in your life, BUT Jesus has come so that you may have life and life in abundance. **Do you believe this promise is for you?**

Let's revisit some of the questions from earlier.
Do you trust God in this? Are you trusting that God can truly restore you, breathe life into you, free you, and transform you? Do you believe that He can do this for you? Do you believe that He wants to do this for you?

If it is hard for you to trust God in this, let's find the why behind it. Is there some hurt lingering? A lie that you believe about yourself or God? Human characteristics that you are placing on God?

Stop here. Take your time with these questions. Close your eyes, take a few deep, slow breaths (in through your nose, out through your mouth), and have a conversation with God about this. Write down anything that comes from that conversation.

*** Since I brought up that I decided to go to counseling after I had met with the surgeon, I must ask you what no one asked me...Do you feel that you may need to see a counselor?
There is absolutely no shame in going to counseling, and it is most likely more normal than you think. God created our brains so amazingly complex, and He also created gifted humans that can help bring you to healing with God's help.

Many times it is simply the unknowns with counseling that stop us from going. It feels scary simply because it is new and different to us. Ask God if counseling may be the direction that He is leading you in.

Homework : Week 2

This week, our focus is on **trusting** and **believing** that God can restore us, heal us, and bring us back to life. It may be difficult for us to believe that God will do this for us and that may be because we don't fully know God's love. I, for so many years, could honestly look you in the eye and tell you that I knew God loved me. Yet, I did not know the kind of love that is described in the Ephesian 3 verses I shared with you earlier. I could not begin to know, "how wide and long and high and deep is the love of Christ, and to know this love that surpasses knowledge" because I was thinking of His love as the Earthly love I knew.

We all have different ways that we have experienced love in our lives. Even if we have experienced a really good, loving relationship, it still is only a sliver of the way God loves us.

Our first activity is to try to get a picture of God's love for us. Take the time to slow yourself down in a quiet spot. Close your eyes and take some deep breaths. Begin to imagine a picture of a loving father. Imagine his eyes and the way he looks at you as if you are his treasure. Imagine a love so big in his eyes, a love that hurts when you hurt, rejoices when you rejoice, and is so very proud of you ALL of the time. As hard as it is, sit here for at least 5 minutes or more if you can.

If this is hard for you, pray Ephesians 3:16-21 over and over again. You can also sit and listen to this playlist I have made all about God's love. Go to this link or scan the QR code at the bottom of the page.
https://tinyurl.com/ykr4787e

This is our Father God. As we begin to see God in this way, through the lens of a perfect love that we cannot fully grasp, but can pray to see more and more clearly, we can begin to trust that He wants what is best for us.

This is who you can put your trust in. This is who you can trust to restore you and breathe life back into you. He created you; He created that seven year old that we looked back on, and He wants that seven year old to be fully alive in you now too. He wants that seven year old to wake up inside of you and come fully alive to the life He always created you for. A life to the FULL!

Each day this week one of the questions to ask yourself is going to be, how can you let God love you today. So often, we are asked how we can love ourselves through self care, but I think a better question to ask is how God wants to love us. This may include simple self care, but it also could include discipline, obedience, confession, forgiveness or even doing one of those things that your seven year old self loved simply to feel pure joy. God's love for us is perfect, so why wouldn't we ask Him how He wants to love on us each day?

Morning Activities and Questions :

Write the answers in a journal each day.
(You can also continue any of the daily questions from last week that you found helpful)

1. **Pray a prayer of trust and surrender each morning. Pray this prayer each morning or write one of your own. As you pray the same words each day, pay attention as your heart changes.**

   Dear God, my desire is to do Your will and to do it willingly, even though my nature and tendency has often been to kick against the pricks of my life circumstances and to try to steer my own course independently of You.

   I pray that by the leading and guidance of the Holy Spirit, I may be willing to present my entire life to You as a sweet smelling aroma.

   Lord, I want to be changed into the person that You want me to be, and to leave behind the things of the flesh, to walk in newness of life, and in spirit and truth with Your Holy Spirit in the driving seat of my life.

   Lord, I want to do what is Your good and acceptable will for my life and to allow Your Holy Spirit to change in me all those fleshly tendencies of life and selfish motives that so often cause me to sin against You. I want to learn obedience through Your teaching work in my life, so that I may be used to bring encouragement to others in thought, word, and motive.

   Keep me from prideful actions and from those little jealous thoughts that so easily tarnish my witness for You, and help me I pray, to develop an attitude of thankfulness and joy in the Lord. May I rejoice always, pray without ceasing, and in everything give thanks to You for Your great goodness to me. Thank you, Lord, for the work that you are doing in me.

   In Jesus' name I pray,
   Amen [3]

2. **How can I let God love me today?**

3. **What is God asking of me today?**
   (Hint: It's usually a lot less than we are asking of ourselves in a day.)

Evening Questions :

1. Where did I take things into my own hands today trying to take control?
2. Where did I let God love me today? Any thoughts after it?

End of the Week :

List ways that God has loved on you this week. What has surprised you about His love?

We Must Take Action

"He said to me, 'Prophecy concerning these bones and say to them…'"
Ezekiel 37:4a

In the first week together, we took the time to discover who God created us to be. We know now that there was once life in us. Then last week, we learned that we need to put our trust fully in God, knowing that He wants what is best for us. His love for us is a perfect love.

As we continue through the coming weeks, let the question, "How can I let God love me?" be on your lips often. Make it a part of your day. Whenever you don't know what to do next, overwhelmed with all that there is to do, emotionally drained, angry, or any time you simply need a reset, notice it. Ask God how you can let Him love you. Then breathe, and listen.

The answers to this question are going to feed into what we are learning this week.

Read through Ezekiel 37: 1-10 again before you go on. Pray for God to show you something new in the text.

Ezekiel 37:4a says,
"He said to me, 'Prophecy concerning these bones and say to them…'"

God was asking Ezekiel to take an active role in bringing the bones back to life. He was asking him to say words over the bones. Did God need Him to do this to bring the bones back to life? No, but He brought Ezekiel into action. Action shows obedience and trust in what God is asking him to do.

We have an active part in our healing. God is asking you to stand up and take part.

As you saw last week, we must first trust. If action comes before trust, then we are simply acting out of our own will and fleshly tendencies. We must first know that God knows best, not us, so that He can call us into action that will lead to healing. It seems easier at times to simply sit back and pray for instant healing when the desperate times come, but many times God is asking us to be obedient in the small tasks leading us through a process of healing. A process that will bring our hearts closer to Him as we go, a process that will train and discipline us to turn towards God when hard times come again, a process that will heal us at the root of the pain, and a process that will show that we trust in Him no matter what He asks of us. The ultimate goal, in all healing, is to be brought closer in relationship to Jesus.

Many times throughout Jesus' life He healed people through a process. I love these stories because He easily could have healed them in an instant, but instead He gave them directions of what to do next to be healed. He was calling them into an active role in the process, growing their trust and strengthening them in obedience.

Look at John 9:1-11

As he was passing by, he saw a man blind from birth. His disciples asked him, "Rabbi, who sinned, this man or his parents, that he was born blind?"

"Neither this man nor his parents sinned," Jesus answered. "This came about so that God's works might be displayed in him. We must do the works of him who sent me while it is day. Night is coming when no one can work. As long as I am in the world, I am the light of the world."

After he said these things he spit on the ground, made some mud from the saliva, and spread the mud on his eyes. "Go," he told him, "wash in the pool of Siloam" (which means "Sent"). So he left, washed, and came back seeing.

His neighbors and those who had seen him before as a beggar said, "Isn't this the one who used to sit begging?" Some said, "He's the one." Others were saying, "No, but he looks like him."

He kept saying, "I'm the one."

So they asked him, "Then how were your eyes opened?"

He answered, "The man called Jesus made mud, spread it on my eyes, and told me, 'Go to Siloam and wash.' So when I went and washed I received my sight."

We could talk about how Jesus said that the blind man was born blind so that God's work could be displayed in him. As hard as it is to acknowledge sometimes, often our struggles are where God's full glory gets to be put on display.

Or we could talk about the name of the pool that Jesus sent him to, which literally means "sent". In our healing process, we are SENT into action.

But what I want us to focus on is that Jesus could have simply said the words, and the man would have been able to see. Jesus could have laid his hands on the man, and his sight would have restored. Instead, Jesus asked something of him. He asked him to go, to wash, and to do this at a specific spot.

Jesus was asking for trust and obedience. He was asking the man to believe, and to act on his belief.

So I must ask...are you sitting and praying for instant healing without also praying for next steps of obedience for healing? Don't stop praying for the instant healing because God CAN and we are fully trusting in his ways. But don't stop there! Pray to know what action He wants you to take. You took a huge step buying this book and beginning the work. Now what is God asking of you next?

Often, when we think of action steps from God, we think they should be given through the clouds opening up and a loud voice from the heavens. We also think that they are going to be these huge steps of calling over our lives. Or we look to others' stories, use mine for example, and only see the beginning where I lost both of my parents and was in the depths of anxiety, and the healing 8 years later. We see it as happening overnight with the loud voice of God and a huge act of obedience on my end. This is not the case.

The steps of obedience God often asks of us are small. Even if they lead to a BIG thing, there are lots of seemingly small steps of obedience to get there. We can't miss them, and we cannot overlook them.

This is also where questions like, "How can I let God love me?" and "How does God want me to grow closer to Him?" can come in handy. These can direct you to what He is asking of you next.

God cares for you, and He truly will give you the steps towards healing. Slowly, one at a time. And oftentimes, He does not give us the next step until we have been obedient in the first. If you feel stuck, look back and ask yourself if you were obedient to the last thing God asked of you.

You may be asking, how can I hear God's voice? Some of the best advice I have ever received was when I asked a mentor, "How do I know if it's God's voice or mine?" She asked me back, "Do you hear it in the quiet or the busyness of your day?"

If it's in the quiet, it is God, and what He says makes my heart race, yet I feel completely calm about it. If it's in the busyness of my day, it is usually my flesh trying to look better, be better, crave recognition or love, or so many other sinful tendencies.

If it is hard for you to know God's voice, take the time to get to know Him better. If you are not around me much, and I called you up on the phone, you would not recognize my voice. But if I was your best friend, you would know my voice from across the room. It is the same with God. The better you know Him, the easier His voice will be to recognize. The more time you spend with Him, the more you will learn His ways and His character through reading the word. The more space you give to Him to speak into your life, the better you will be at recognizing when He is speaking to you.

GOD'S VOICE	SATAN'S VOICE
CALMS	OBSESSES
COMFORTS	WORRIES
CONVICTS	CONDEMNS
ENCOURAGES	DISCOURAGES
ENLIGHTENS	CONFUSES
LEADS	PUSHES
REASSURES	FRIGHTENS
STILLS	RUSHES

I used to think that God was only after my spiritual life, my inner being, my mind and my heart. As I grew in listening to God's voice, I began to realize He had a lot to say about how I was feeding and caring for my body also. He cared about my body more than I ever knew!

I Corinthians 6:19-20 says,
"Don't you know that your body is a temple of the Holy Spirit who is in you, whom you have from God? You are not your own, for you were bought at a price. So glorify God with your body."

Elisabeth Elliot says,
"We cannot give our hearts to God and keep our bodies to ourselves."[1]

There are many times in the Bible where God directs people in how they care for their body. The body can become a major distraction when we do not care for it well. Pain, anxiety, sluggishness, exhaustion, and so many other bodily distractions can stem from how we are taking care of our body. Our body can distract us from growing in our relationship with Jesus and from doing the work that He is asking of us.

In 1 Kings 19, we see that Elijah is on the run, afraid for his life.

Read verses 4-8.
"...but he went on a day's journey into the wilderness. He sat down under a broom tree and prayed that he might die. He said, 'I have had enough! Lord, take my life, for I'm no better than my ancestors.' Then he lay down and slept under the broom tree.

Suddenly, an angel touched him. The angel told him, 'Get up and eat.' Then he looked, and there at his head was a loaf of bread baked over hot stones, and a jug of water. So he ate and drank and lay down again. Then the angel of the Lord returned for a second time and touched him. He said, 'Get up and eat, or the journey will be too much for you.' So he got up, ate, and drank. Then on the strength from that food, he walked forty days and forty nights to Horeb, the mountain of God. He entered a cave there and spent the night."

I love what Ruth Haley Barton says about this piece of scripture in her book Sacred Rhythms.

"...I was struck by the attention God gave to Elijah's physical condition, going so far as to send an angel to guide him in caring for his body. I was comforted to find that even though Elijah was a great prophet, he had the same blind spot I was beginning to acknowledge in myself: he had let himself become so run down that God had to send an angel to strengthen his body before they could deal with anything else. The angel helped him pay attention to the condition of his body as the vehicle that would enable him to take the journey that lay ahead. The angel even pointed out that if he did not care for his body, the journey into the presence of God would be too much for him."[2]

In much of my healing journey, God has asked me for obedience in how I care for my body. I want to point this out because as you are listening to what He wants next for you this week, it may be something to do with your heart or mind, but it also may be something to do with your body or health.

He didn't ask this of me all at once, it was a slow process over years, but here are some areas that He has led me to:
- Revelation Wellness' Podcast and then also their RevWell TV workouts. [3] I began to workout out of kindness to my body instead of always pushing my body to be better.
- Sugar Fast - I did a full Sugar Fast that God placed in my lap and out of it realized how much sugar spiked my anxiety. Even the littlest of amounts.
- Caffeine - I had a health scare over a year ago and for some of the tests they recommended that I cut out all caffeine. Then my doctor said that she would recommend staying off of it. (This was so hard! But it doesn't mean that it wasn't good.) Then I began noticing again, less anxiety.

With food, it is important to note **1 Corinthians 6:12.**

'**"Everything is permissible for me," but not everything is beneficial. "Everything is permissible for me," but I will not be mastered by anything.'**

The food that may not be good for me, may be fine for you, and vice versa. Everything is permissible, but if it begins to master us, if we begin to go to it emotionally instead of to God, then we may need to ask Him how we should approach this food for now. We also need to be willing to be obedient if He asks us to give it up for a while.

There have been so many other ways that God has taught me how to care for my body that He created, but more than anything, I have seen that when I follow His guidance, I have more energy to do what He has asked of me. I know that He needs my mind and body focused and clear to love and teach the people He has put in my life. But even more importantly, I need my mind and body strong to enter into the presence of God. As the angel of the Lord (which is believed to be Jesus) came to Elijah, he said, "Get up and eat, or the journey will be too much for you." If we are honest, when our body has pain, discomfort, fatigue, or haziness of mind it can be hard for us to "journey" into the presence of God. We seem to not have the energy for it. Yet when we are getting enough sleep, eating well, drinking lots of water, and moving our bodies we have a clarity that comes. It becomes easier for us to choose to be in God's presence throughout the day instead of checking out through entertainment or food to ignore our hurting bodies.

I cannot say all this without saying that the world wants us to worship our bodies, but instead we are called to worship God IN OUR BODIES. There is a difference. If our "why" behind working out and eating healthy is to reach a certain perfection with our body, a certain weight or look, then we may be worshiping our bodies.

1 Corinthians 10:31 says,
"So, whether you eat or drink, or whatever you do, do everything for the glory of God."

This is our new WHY. We are going to take our physical health to Him and be obedient in what He asks of us, "FOR THE GLORY OF GOD".

What is God asking you to do next? Where do you need to be obedient and step up into action? Throughout the week, take time to be with Him, listen to Him, and then begin taking action. We may not always know why He is asking something of us, but TRUST that it will be FOR HIS GLORY and that no obedience is wasted.

Homework : Week 3

We are going to take ACTION this week. Here are your ACTION STEPS:

1. **"This is the day that the Lord has made, I will rejoice and be glad in it."**

When you wake up, practice saying these words first thing, the second you open your eyes. Either say it in your head or actually say it out loud (speaking words out loud holds so much power). Make this part of your morning routine.

2. **Make getting into The Word your FIRST THING.**

Before Instagram, before Facebook, before email, before the news, FIRST!
We need the filter of God's lens before we go out into the world each morning.

So this leads to the question, do you need to wake up a little earlier to be able to do this? We are going to talk more about reading our bibles next week, but here are some simple resources to get started if you do not have a plan. Pick something and do not overcomplicate it.

- The Bible Recap
- Write the Word Journal by Cultivate What Matters
- Read through the book of John, chapter by chapter or section by small section.
- Holy Bible App has many reading plans to choose from.

3. **Be grateful!**
Write 3 things that you're grateful for each morning this week. Get specific. Don't simply write down family, but write down that you are thankful for the way your family helped one another clean up the kitchen after dinner or the way your child hugs you first thing in the morning. As we get more specific, we begin to see the goodness of God all over our days.

4. **Move your body every day!**
Don't panic! This does not mean that you need to do a strenuous workout every day. Walk as you listen to a Reving the Word Podcast or worship music or scripture, or walk and be in prayer or silence. Stretch. If you have a foam roller, roll your body before bed or first thing in the morning. Do 5 minutes of jumping jacks, air jump rope, high knees and marching in place. Go up and down the stairs 10 times. Simply make the choice for movement every day. This is a way to get your anxious energy out and renew your mind along with so many physical benefits. And if you choose to listen to one of the podcasts while you are moving, you get the added bonus of setting your mind on Truth, which will literally renew your mind.

5. **Continue sitting with God asking what your next step of obedience is.**
If you know what it is, DO IT! Let your prayer partner know if you need some encouragement.

Resource Links for Week 3 :

The Bible Recap

http://www.thebiblerecap.com/start

Write the Word Journal

https://cultivatewhatmatters.com/
collections/faith

Reving the Word Podcast

https://www.revelationwellness.org/
workout/podcast-2/

Hear the Word of the Lord

"Dry bones, hear the word of the Lord!"
Ezekiel 37: 4b

Let's look back before we begin this week. In week one, we took the time to recognize that there was once life in us. During week two, we chose to trust and believe that God will breathe life back into us. Last week, we took action!

What's our next step?

Before we begin, take the time to read through Ezekiel 37: 1-10 again. You might want to choose to read it from a different version than what you have been reading it from. Maybe choose a paraphrase version of the bible like the Message.

Ezekiel 37: 4b says,
"Dry bones, hear the word of the Lord!"

This is what God told Ezekiel to say over the bones. Hear the word of the Lord. The word of God is POWERFUL! It is powerful enough to bring dry bones back to life. It is powerful enough to bring the dead back to life. HIS WORD IS POWERFUL! **Let's not miss this! I'm going to let you in on a little secret...you have direct access to God's words!**
THE BIBLE!

I think one reason why we struggle getting into the Word is because we simply take it for granted. I would bet that we all have a Bible. We may even have multiple copies in our houses. We have the Bible on our phones. We can even listen to the Bible being read to us. The amount of access we have seems as if it should make it super easy for us to read the Bible, but maybe the access that we have to the Bible makes it seem less valuable and less powerful to us.

Let's not forget what the Bible is...

2 Timothy 3:16-17 says,
"All Scripture is breathed out by God and profitable for teaching, for reproof, for correction, and for training in righteousness, that the man of God may be complete, equipped for every good work." (ESV)

Hebrews 4:12 says,
"For the word of God is living and effective and sharper than any double-edged sword, penetrating as far as the separation of soul and spirit, joints and marrow. It is able to judge the thoughts and intentions of the heart."

Matthew 4:4 says,
" He answered, 'It is written: Man must not live on bread alone but on every word that comes from the mouth of God.'"

Psalm 119:105 says,
"Your word is a lamp for my feet and a light on my path."

Proverbs 30:5 says,
"Every word of God proves true; he is a shield to those who take refuge in him." (ESV)

Isaiah 40:8 says,
"The grass withers, the flowers fade, but the word of our God remains forever."

Have we forgotten that the Bible is actually God's words? If you feel like you cannot hear the voice of God, open your Bible because THEY ARE ALL HIS WORDS! And as we saw in Ezekiel, GOD'S WORDS HAVE POWER! You can see in all of the verses above what God's word can do.

The Bible wasn't created to simply inform us, but to TRANSFORM us!

We must be in God's word. It is where the power is! It is where we will find TRUTH, about God and about ourselves. His word is still living and active.

As we have already learned, the more we are in our Bibles, the better we will be at recognizing God's voice. We will be able to discern quicker whether it is our desire of the flesh speaking or if it is God. We will be able to recognize lies from the enemy quicker. And we will be able to put our trust in God more easily because we will know His true character.

None of this happens overnight. It takes time. I'll never forget sitting around a table with women that I deeply respected because of their faith and trust in Jesus. I only had a few years under my belt with Jesus, and the way they talked about the word of God did not sound like how I was experiencing the word of God. They loved it, and they desired it! When they quoted scripture or spoke of a biblical story, it didn't sound boring. It sounded as if it was modern and alive.

They made me want to read my bible, but I was impatient. I wanted what they had within a week or at least in a couple of months. I even thought how great it would be if I could take a little USB Flash Drive, plug it into them, download everything they knew about the Bible, and then download it into me.

This is where we run into the same problem that I spoke of before. The Bible wasn't created to simply inform us, but to TRANSFORM us! Even if I could download everything they knew about the Bible, I wouldn't speak of it with the joy that these older women did. Why? Because I hadn't lived it. I wouldn't have been the one that grabbed my Bible even on the days I didn't want to. On the days where everything was great and yet I still chose to be in the word. On the days when I was desperate for hope. On the days when my mind was spinning and I begged God to slow it down. On the days that I didn't understand His will for my life or how the worst could happen when He was supposedly a good God.

No one else can make the Bible a treasure for us. It will only become a treasure when we have chosen to sit and read it, day in and day out, over many years. It takes time, but it is so worth it.

A wise friend told me the other day that we first read our Bibles out of duty, then duty turns into discipline, then slowly discipline turns into desire, and then desire turns into delight. I pray that we will all experience desiring and delighting in God's word. But let me also tell you this, when reading the Bible is out of duty or discipline, it is not wasted time. God does not waste obedience. Even if you don't see it right away, I promise you He is using it in you and those around you.

Not only does the Bible tell us the Truth about God, but it also tells us the Truth about ourselves. I don't know about you, but I no longer want to believe what others think of me, what the world thinks of me, what I think about myself, and especially what the enemy thinks of me. I want to only believe what is true, what God thinks of me. This changes everything. **THIS IS WHERE WE ARE SET FREE!**

Romans 8:5-6 says,
"For those who live according to the flesh have their minds set on things of the flesh, but those who live according to the Spirit have their minds set on the things of the Spirit. Now the mind-set of the flesh is death, but the mind-set of the Spirit is life and peace."

2 Corinthians 10:3-5 says,
"For although we live in the flesh, we do not wage war according to the flesh, since the weapons of our warfare are not of the flesh, but are powerful through God for the demolition of strongholds. We demolish arguments and every proud thing that is raised up against the knowledge of God, and we take every thought captive to obey Christ."

The Message Version of this says, "We use our powerful God-tools for smashing warped philosophies, tearing down barriers erected against the truth of God, fitting every loose thought and emotion and impulse into the structure of life shaped by Christ."

So what are our God-tools to get rid of the lies that we so often believe? They are simpler than you think, yet take discipline to actually do. It is what the people of the world would call positive self-talk, yet we would call a mind set on the Spirit. There are so many Spiritual Disciplines that the world has stolen and taken God out of, and somehow we have forgotten that they were God's good idea for our health and wellness from the very beginning. Let's put God back into our positive self-talk and set our minds on the Spirit.

This is where we need to take action. **We need to take our reading of God's word and put the words to actual work in our lives.**

We first must recognize the lies that we are believing. This may take some time. Before you even begin your homework this week, you will need to begin recognizing the lies. Have a piece of paper or notes on your phone, and throughout the day notice what you are telling yourself.

These lies may be hard to recognize at first, especially if the lies have become so ingrained that you now see them as truth (this is why we have to be in The Word so that we can begin to recognize the difference between Truth and lies).

We are aware every day of our conscious mind.
- **The conscious mind** contains all of the thoughts, memories, feelings, and wishes of which we are aware at any given moment. This is the aspect of our mental processing that we can think and talk about rationally.

We are going to have to become aware of our unconscious mind.
- **The unconscious mind** is a reservoir of feelings, thoughts, urges, and memories that are outside of our conscious awareness. Most of the contents of the unconscious are unacceptable or unpleasant, such as feelings of pain, anxiety, or conflict.[1]

The unconscious mind is where the lies are. It's time to turn them into Truth! The Bible tells us that we can renew our minds.

Romans 12:2 says,
"Do not be conformed to this age, but be transformed by the renewing of your mind, so that you may discern what is the good, pleasing, and perfect will of God."

Science is finally starting to catch up with the Bible in this. Dr. Caroline Leaf, a neuroscientist and Christian, says, "Neuroplasticity by definition means the brain is malleable and adaptable, changing moment by moment of every day. Scientists are finally beginning to see the brain as having renewable characteristics (as in Rom. 12:2); it is no longer viewed as a machine that is hardwired early in life, unable to adapt, and wearing out with age."[2]

This means that as we recognize the lies that we believe and make the conscious effort to change them into Truth, we will actually change our brains and renew our minds. The more we do this, the more we will notice our brains not going to the lies but to Truth first.

Jennie Allen has said, "When you and I choose to believe a lie about ourselves, it's one of these three lies we believe: I'm helpless. I'm worthless. I'm unlovable."[3] Most of our specific, personal lies boil down to one of these three. The main lie that whispers to me throughout so many painful situations is that I am unlovable. It shows up when I get upset that a family member doesn't show interest in who I am or what I'm doing. It shows up when my husband simply chooses to go do something instead of sit with me. It shows up when I feel uninvited. It shows up when I am not reaching perfection especially when I feel like someone is critiquing me. It shows up in so many ways, but it always whispers the same thing...you are unloveable.

Here's the truth that I replace this lie with every time I recognize it's whisper.
I AM LOVED. I AM CHOSEN. HE DELIGHTS IN ME.

I have made this into a mantra, a prayer, a positive self-talk, or better yet, words to set my mind on the Spirit. I say it over and over again until it begins to sink in. I say it until I remember how loved I really am. I say it until what I am begging for from other people is fulfilled through my relationship with the only One who can give me the love I am craving.

All this to say, we are going to root out the lies you are believing. We are going to replace them with Truth, and we are going to renew our minds this week. The power that God's word has over our lives is HUGE! It is like nothing else. **It is about time that we use it to its full potential to set us free!**

Tips for Getting and Staying in God's Word :

Here are some tips to help you get in the word and stay in the word. This is the first place the enemy will try to distract. It is an all out war every day to choose to be reading God's word. We have to treat it as a battle and have a plan ready. Make the choice to fight because it becomes even scarier if you begin not caring whether or not you are reading God's word. This is apathy. This is when we know the devil has taken ground in our lives.

01 Remember that it is God's word. This is literally God speaking to you, and you have access to this! Incredible! (2 Timothy 3:16-17)

02 Expect that God will move when you read His word. Be open to the Holy Spirit. (Hebrews 4:12)

03 Pray before you begin reading.
   a. God, give me knowledge and understanding.
   b. God, help me to see something new about You.
   c. God, correct any lies that I believe about You or myself, or anything that I misunderstand.
   d. God, direct my steps according to Your Word.

04 Pick two translations. Pick one that is as close to the original translation as possible while being able to enjoy and understand what you are reading. I enjoy the CSB translation. Then pick another one that is more of a paraphrase in everyday language, such as The Passion or The Message translations . This will bring new life, joy, and understanding to the words if they have become dry.

05 Have a plan. Know what you are going to read. When we sit down with our Bibles in the morning without a plan, we can get lost and distracted pretty quickly. Find a study or simply choose a book of the Bible, and slowly read through it.

06   Make it a daily habit. It doesn't always have to look like the perfect Instagram worthy "quiet time". Simply choose a time of day that works for you, and commit to it. After sticking to it at the same time daily for a few weeks, it will become a habit.

07   Make it your FIRST priority. Often we will say that it is our most important thing, but our screen time tells us differently. Make the choice now that it is your first priority. It is your most important commitment on your calendar every day.

08   Use additional resources. Don't understand something or want to simply understand it at a deeper level? There are so many resources at our fingertips. Blue Letter Bible is a great one. [4]

09   Read to Understand. Even though we will never understand everything in the Bible, make the effort when you are reading to find out more. Make sure to understand the context in which you are reading. This is why I like to read through books of the Bible. Before I read the book, I read about the timeline, the background, and the message and purpose in my bible. I also watch The Bible Project [5] book overview videos.

10   Ask Questions. As you are reading ask:
    a. What does this teach me about God?
    b. What does this teach me about how I should live?
    c. What stands out to me from this text?
    d. God, what are you saying to me today through this?
    e. God, what do you want me to do with this today?

11 Write Scripture Out. With at least one verse in my reading each day, I will write it out in my notebook. There is something about how it deepens my understanding, and it always sinks into my heart as I write it out.

12 Journal out your prayers, feelings, or thoughts after reading. This is a great way to have a conversation with God. The slowness of my pen to paper gives Him space to talk to me.

13 Have an accountability partner. Ask a friend to check in on you. Talk to a friend about what you are reading. The best thing for me is to have the app Voxer. Daily I talk with a few different friends about what we are reading. It definitely keeps me accountable.

14 Persevere. There are going to be days you miss. Don't let the day or two turn into weeks. Jump back in. You are not a failure for missing a few days.

15 Be okay with each day looking a little different. Some days you'll read a verse, and some days you'll read a chapter. Some days will be for soaking and sitting with the Lord over a single verse, while some days will be for deep study. You will not be doing each one of these tips each day. Look at your Bible reading through the lens of an entire week and an entire month. The key is to simply get in the Word in some way each day. Each day may just look different than the last.

My Identity in Jesus

BELOVED
"I have loved you with an everlasting love;
therefore, I have continued to extend faithful love to you."
- Jeremiah 31:3

A CHILD OF GOD
"See what great love the Father has given us that we should be called God's children—and we are!" - 1 John 3:1

DELIGHTED IN
"The Lord your God is among you, a warrior who saves. He will rejoice over you with gladness. He will be quiet in his love. He will delight in you with singing." - Zephaniah 3:17

FORGIVEN
"He himself bore our sins in his body on the tree; so that, having died to sins, we might live for righteousness. By his wounds you have been healed." - 1 Peter 2:24

WASHED CLEAN
"Though your sins are scarlet, they will be as white as snow; though they are crimson red, they will be like wool." - Isaiah 1:18

FREE
"For freedom, Christ set us free. Stand firm, then, and don't submit again to a yoke of slavery." - Galations 5:1

A TEMPLE OF THE HOLY SPIRIT
"Don't you know that your body is a temple of the Holy Spirit who is in you, whom you have from God?" - 1 Corinthians 6:19

ADOPTED BY GOD'S FAMILY
"You received the Spirit of adoption, by whom we cry out, "Abba, Father!" - Romans 8:15

CO-HEIR WITH CHRIST
"And if children, also heirs—heirs of God and coheirs with Christ" - Romans 8:17

RIGHTEOUS
"He made the one who did not know sin to be sin for us, so that in him we might become the righteousness of God."
- 2 Corinthians 5:21

NEW
"Therefore, if anyone is in Christ, he is a new creation; the old has passed away, and see, the new has come!"
- 2 Corinthians 5:17

SET APART
"You are a chosen race, a royal priesthood, a holy nation, a people for his possession." - 1 Peter 2:9

AN AMBASSADOR OF CHRIST
"Therefore, we are ambassadors for Christ, since God is making his appeal through us." - 2 Corinthians 5:20

A CO-LABORER
"For we are God's coworkers. You are God's field, God's building." - 1 Corinthians 3:9

A SWEET AROMA
"For we are to God the pleasing aroma of Christ among those who are being saved and those who are perishing."
- 2 Corinthians 2:15 (NIV)

NEVER ALONE
"The Lord is the one who will go before you. He will be with you; he will not leave you or abandon you." - Deuteronomy 31:8

A MASTERPIECE
"For we are God's masterpiece. He has created us anew in Christ Jesus, so we can do the good things he planned for us long ago." - Ephesians 2:10 (NLT)

WONDERFULLY MADE
"I am fearfully and wonderfully made." - Psalm 139:14 (NIV)

BOLD
"Since, then, we have such a hope, we act with great boldness."
- 2 Corinthians 3:12

HAVING GUARANTEED VICTORY
"You have given me your shield of victory. Your right hand supports me; your help has made me great." - Psalm 18:35 (NLT)

HOLDING A SECURED FUTURE
" For I know the plans I have for you"—this is the Lord's declaration—"plans for your well-being, not for disaster, to give you a future and a hope." - Jeremiah 29:11

WHOLE IN CHRIST
"In Christ you have been brought to fullness."
- Colossians 2:10 (NIV)

Homework : Week 4

1. **"My Identity in Jesus"**
   a. Read through it.
   b. Pick one or two that Jesus is speaking over you. These are probably the ones that are hard to believe about yourself or ones that make you uncomfortable.
   c. Sit with Him and ask why this Truth is hard for you to hear. Take time to journal this out.
   d. Write the word or words of identity on a sticky note, and put it somewhere that you will see throughout each day this week.
   e. Continue to say it out loud over yourself throughout the week. Speak the Truth to yourself.

2. **Set Our Minds On Truth**
   a. First, write down some of the lies that you believe about yourself. These may not make sense to you because your rational mind could explain why these are not true about you, but your subconscious is telling you this lie over and over. It doesn't matter if it is rational or not. If this lie is popping up often, take the time to recognize it so that we can change it.
   b. Choose one lie that you wrote down and change it into a truth.
      i. The lie: I am not worth it..nothing will ever change.
      ii. Truth: I am valuable and God is making me new.
   c. Find scripture to back up your truth with God's word.
      i. I am valuable. / Matthew 6:26 "Consider the birds of the sky: They don't sow or reap or gather into barns, yet your heavenly Father feeds them. Aren't you worth more than they?"
      ii. God is making me new. / Isaiah 43:18-19 "'Do not remember the past events; pay no attention to things of old. Look, I am about to do something new; even now it is coming. Do you not see it? Indeed, I will make a way in the wilderness, rivers in the desert.'"
   d. Take more of the lies that you have written down and take the time to turn them into truths backed up by scripture. Write it all out.
   e. Let's take this even farther. Let's not stop here. As we have been saying, there is power in our words, power in the words of God, and power in the spoken word. Hopefully now you have 3-5 new truths written down. Download a Voice Recording App. I have one called "Voice Memos". Record yourself saying these truths and quoting the scriptures. This is how I do it. I speak the truth once, pause, then speak the truth again, then read the scripture. Once you record them all on one voice recording, then you will be able to listen back to them each morning.

As you are listening, you'll hear the first time you state the truth statement, then as you hear it a second time you will repeat it out loud along with your voice recording.

Words are so very powerful. Trust me when I say, listening to this daily will change and renew your mind. Then add movement such as walking with it and watch out! Your mind will change!

Here is another amazing resource for you to pull from to find your Truths.
https://www.valmariepaper.com/embracing-biblical-view-affirmations/

Let the Breath of the Holy Spirit Breathe Into You

"This is what the Lord God says to these bones: I will cause breath to enter you, and you will live."
Ezekiel 37:5

You have come so far! I am so proud of you! Let's take another look back at where we have been. We now…

- Recognize that there was once life in us.
- Trust that God will breathe life back into us.
- Can step up and take action.
- Begin to see the power of God's Word and Truth over our lives.

This week, we are going to let the breath of the Holy Spirit breathe into us!

Again, open your Bible, and read Ezekiel 37:1-10. Go slow, breathe deep breaths, and read it out loud.

**Ezekiel 37:5 says, "This is what the Lord God says to these bones:
I will cause breath to enter you, and you will live."**

Take a deep, slow breath. Slowly take four deep breaths, in through the nose and out through the mouth. Nice and slow. Relax your shoulders away from your ears. Close your eyes. Enjoy the deep breaths.

There is something to the breath, isn't there? Again, there is both science and scripture behind the breath and what makes it so good for us.

Here are some of the benefits from deep breathing:
1. Decreases stress, increases calm.
2. Relieves pain.
3. Stimulates the lymphatic system (Detoxifies the body).
4. Improves immunity.
5. Increases energy.
6. Lowers blood pressure.
7. Improves digestion.[1]

Long before we understood the science behind breath, God showed us the importance of breath.

**In Genesis 2:7 it says,
"Then the Lord God formed the man out of the dust from the ground and breathed the breath of
life into his nostrils, and the man became a living being."**

**Job 33:4 says,
"The Spirit of God has made me, and the breath of the Almighty gives me life."**

He created us with the power of His breath. The first air into our nostrils was the breath of God. Each breath we take is because of Him!

I love the verses after Jesus has risen from the dead, and He is with His disciples.
   In John 20:22 it says, **"After saying this, he breathed on them and said, 'Receive the Holy Spirit.'"**

Whether you believe that Jesus was actually giving them the Holy Spirit in some measure here or simply promising that the Holy Spirit would come to them later (Pentecost), Jesus breathed on them. This would have represented new life to them knowing that this was the same way Adam was given life. I have to wonder, did the disciples take a deep slow inhale? What a glorious breath!

Are we taking slow enough breaths to take the time to allow the Holy Spirit to work in us? Do we even know what that means?

For so long, I ignored the Holy Spirit. I could wrap my brain around God and Jesus, but because the Holy Spirit felt so unexplainable to me, I ignored this piece of God. I don't think I'm the only one.

I was missing out on the power and love of God in the way that can only be given through His Spirit! I was missing out on the guidance that the Holy Spirit gives us in the everyday. I was missing out on the inner work of conviction, teaching, and sanctifying that the Holy Spirit provides.

Do we realize what we are missing out on?

In the book, Forgotten God by Francis Chan, he says,
"Jesus Himself said to His disciples, 'It is for your good that I am going away. Unless I go away, the Counselor will not come to you; but if I go, I will send him to you' (John 16:7 NIV). So Jesus is basically telling His disciples, 'Yes, I was with you for three and a half years, but it is better that I leave you and the Holy Spirit comes to you.'

When the disciples heard that two thousand years ago, I'm sure it was hard for them to grasp. How could it be better to trade a human Jesus - a man they could talk and eat and laugh with - for a Spirit they couldn't physically see? Thousands of years later, I think most of us would also choose a physical Jesus over an invisible Spirit. But what do we do with the fact that Jesus says it is better for His followers to have the Holy Spirit? Do we believe Him? If so, do our lives reflect that belief?"

Can you imagine Jesus walking alongside us throughout every day? Loving on us, delighting in us, seeing us, guiding us, closing our mouths when they need closed, encouraging us, cheering us on when we need to be bold, telling us how to act in our relationships, and directing our path each moment of every day. It sounds incredible!

Jesus says we have something that is better!! The Holy Spirit!

The Holy Spirit...
- Helps us
- Teaches us
- Comforts us
- Encourages us
- Advises us
- Strengthens us
- Frees us
- Loves us
- Convicts us
- Produces fruit in us
- Guides us into Truth
- Leads us to intimacy with God
- Fills us with hope
- Gives us all the Fruit of the Spirit
- Heals us
- Restores us

The Holy Spirit does the work in us. He does the heavy lifting. He does the work of healing like we could never do on our own.

The Holy Spirit can only do what we allow Him to do though. We need to make space for Him to work. We need to sit in His presence and open up to His voice and His leading. This is where we lose all control. It is no longer reading The Word and checking it off the list. This is where we have to sit and be in relationship. This is where we have to allow deep intimacy. This is where we often get scared.

What if I hear nothing? What if the Holy Spirit does nothing in me? What if the power of the Holy Spirit is for other people more qualified and not for me? What if He's not real? This again is where our trust needs to come into play. This is where we need to know we have a faithful God.

This is when we repeat the verse Jeremiah 29:13,
"You will seek me and find me when you search for me with all your heart."

Or in the Message paraphrase it says,
"When you come looking for me, you'll find me. Yes, when you get serious about finding me and want it more than anything else, I'll make sure you won't be disappointed."

You will find Him if you are looking for Him. You will not be disappointed!

Or maybe the fear is what if He is real and asks for something I don't want to give? Or convicts us of our sin and we don't want to change? Or challenges us in areas that we would rather stay apathetic?

We will never be free if we are not willing to surrender to Him. We will never be free if we cannot confess our sins as the Holy Spirit convicts us. What may feel hard and tender to go through is many times necessary to free ourselves from what is entangling us in the first place.

1 John 1:9 says,
"If we confess our sins, he is faithful and righteous to forgive us our sins
and to cleanse us from all unrighteousness."

We do not have to be afraid of this because it says in **Psalm 16:11,**
"…in your presence is abundant joy…"

Let us not forget the loving God that we have.

This week we are going to make space for the Holy Spirit in our lives. We are going to welcome Him in. We are going to begin or deepen our intimacy with Him.

I am going to give you direction by showing you ways to slow down to welcome the Holy Spirit, but I am by no means going to box the Holy Spirit into only these activities that I am giving to you. The Holy Spirit can work in your life in any way He choses! I am simply going to give you tangible ways to welcome Him into your daily life. We have got to make space!

One of the ways that we are going to make space for the Holy Spirit is Breath Prayer. Adele Ahlberg Calhoun says, "Breathing is an unconscious thing. And breath prayer reminds us that just as we can't live on one breath of air, we can't live on one breath of God. God is the oxygen of our soul, and we need to breathe him in all day long. After all, it is in him that 'we live and move and have our being' (Acts 17:28). Breath prayer reminds us that each breath we are given is God's gift and that God's Spirit is nearer to us than our own breath."[2]

A simple practice of Breath Prayer begins by breathing in calling on a biblical name or image of God, and breathing out stating a simple God-given desire.

So you sit. You breathe in deep as you say the name of God that is special to you, and you exhale as you voice your prayer. Some examples being…
- Breathe in "Healer", breathe out "speak the word and I shall be healed."
- Breathe in "Father", breathe out "let your love fill me."
- Breathe in "Lord", breathe out "here I am."

As you practice this, you will make space for the Holy Spirit to work deep in you, and you will begin to see that you can practice this anytime and anywhere throughout your day. If you want to learn more about Breath Prayer, I highly recommend that you go and watch this video from Revelation Wellness. (https://www.revelationwellness.org/livestream-breathprayer/)

More than anything, with each of these exercises, learn to be expectant and lean into the discomfort. We get uncomfortable even talking about the Holy Spirit because we fear what He may stir in us, and we cannot control His activity in our life. We also get uncomfortable because it is hard to explain when He has done something in our life. The Holy Spirit often works beyond our words to the depth of our very own heart.

"We see how the Spirit worked in the early church, how He guided and empowered believers, and rather than be excited by such activity, we're frightened. We find it more comfortable to keep God at arm's length, to focus on Him doctrinally rather than experientially, because we're afraid He will call us to step out of our comfort zone."[3] As we say in Revelation Wellness, **let's get comfortable being uncomfortable.**

THIS IS WHERE THE JOY IS!

THIS IS WHERE THE FREEDOM IS!

THIS IS WHERE WE BEGIN TO HAVE A LIFE TO THE FULLNESS THAT JESUS PROMISES!

We also tend to look back on times that we thought we felt, saw, or heard the Holy Spirit moving in our life, and we begin to doubt it because we have downplayed it. In the moment, we know without a doubt when the Holy Spirit has moved our hearts, but then we look back on it and start to ask, am I sure that was really the Holy Spirit? Or we tell a friend about it, and as we tell it, there are never words to fully explain how it felt so we begin to lose the depth of the experience.

This is where we need to write it all down. We must keep our stones of remembrance so that we will not forget when and how the Holy Spirit moved in our lives.[4] If the Israelites can begin to doubt that God is looking out for them right after He parts the Red Sea to get them to safety, I have to believe that we will forget too.

Let's be willing to get uncomfortable this week. Let's expect the Holy Spirit to move in our lives. This is where we will COME TO LIFE!

Homework : Week 5

Try a few or all of these practices. Each one is meant to make space for the Holy Spirit. Test them out and see where God speaks. The one that God is asking you to do may not be the most comfortable one for you. Most likely, it will be uncomfortable.

Breath Prayer :
Practice Breath Prayer each day. Maybe look back to the Truths from last week to see what you need your breath prayer to focus on. Use this practice in the morning first thing, at times where you can sit and simply be with God, and also throughout your day in the midst of daily life. It may be a good practice to set a few alarms on your phone to remind you to do the breath prayer throughout the day.

Be Still :
It is so hard to simply be still. Meditation is another practice that the world has removed God out of, but we are going to put Him back into it. Meditation allows us to fully pay attention and for God to instill His truth and love into us.

There are many ways to do this. One of the ways described in the Spiritual Disciplines Handbook is this…
"To meditate on Scripture choose a verse, chapter or book of the Bible. Don't hurry. Listen to the Scripture. Write down your questions. Use your imagination. You may wish to memorize a short part of the text to keep it clearly before you. Like a cow chewing the cud, keep returning to your text with your mind and heart. When you are distracted, gently return to your text. Express once again your desire to pay attention."[4]

You can also simply listen to a worship song over and over again sitting still and comfortably. You can focus on an attribute of God and ask Him questions. You can focus on His creation. Whatever you do, it is simply setting aside the time to just BE WITH HIM.

If you struggle to start this on your own, go and listen to this Be Still & Be Loved (https://tinyurl.com/ktrh85d6) offered by Revelation Wellness.
They have many of the Be Still & Be Loved podcasts
that you can choose from.

Prayer :
Make prayer a practice this week. Choose to set aside time to pray. This is our conversation with God. This is where we get to be in relationship with Him. It helps me to write out my prayers sometimes, but don't make this work. It is a joy to be able to talk with Him.

If you struggle to bring prayer into your daily life, Val Woerner has some amazing resources! Here is a free resource that she offers with prayer prompts for different rooms in your house. (https://tinyurl.com/crpxxsyy)

Or simply pray over a certain area each day: community, church, family, friends, and yourself.

Walk or move in some way as you listen to a Revelation Wellness Lectio Divina Podcast :
Here is one (https://tinyurl.com/7ayfyp9h), but there are many to choose from.

These are POWERFUL! This is a guided conversation with the Holy Spirit. I was so extremely uncomfortable when I did one of these for the first time. I worried about exactly what we talked about earlier, that I would hear nothing. But every time that I have gone in with a heart expectant and willing to be in the discomfort, the Holy Spirit has spoken to me in magnificent ways! I encourage you to try it!

— WEEK —

6

Obey What He Is Asking of You

"So I prophesied as I had been commanded. While I was prophesying, there was a noise, a rattling sound, and the bones came together, bone to bone."
Ezekiel 37:7

Welcome to Week 6! Can you believe it?! Let's look back again and remind ourselves of where we have been together. We have...

- Recognized that there was once life in us.
- Trusted that God will breathe life back into us.
- Chosen to step up and take action.
- Began to see the power of God's Word and Truth over our lives.
- Allowed the Holy Spirit to breathe into us.

This week we are going to obey what He is asking of us!

First, let us again read Ezekiel 37:1-10. I know you have read it through at least six times at this point, but let us remember that God's Word never returns void to us. His word has power! Pray that he would reveal something to you that you have not seen before today.

Ezekiel 37:7 says,
"So I prophesied as I had been commanded. While I was prophesying, there was a noise,
a rattling sound, and the bones came together, bone to bone."

Ezekiel did what God asked Him to do. God asked him to speak the words, and he did it. Ezekiel was obedient to exactly what God was asking of him.

This may seem like a small thing as we are reading it, but is it? I know that in my life, it is not. Have you ever had the pounding in your chest, heart racing, knowing that God is asking you to say something to someone? Or have you ever had the Holy Spirit whisper to you to keep your mouth shut about something? Saying words that God has asked of us or keeping our mouths shut when He asks us to be quiet is not an easy task.

There are so many times that I have been disobedient to God in this. Sadly, more than I even know. I have even chosen to disobey at times knowing that I had heard His voice guiding me, but I did not want to do it or chose to do what felt good in my flesh. I did what felt easier. It breaks my heart to think about all that I may have missed out on.

But, there have also been times where I boldly chose to say what He had asked of me.

Recently, I had a wave of boldness and was praying over and over for God to use me to speak into people's lives. I asked Him to give me words straight from Him for others. This was an "anything" (oh, Lord, I will do anything) prayer. "Anything" prayers can be terrifying. God wasted no time answering.

I had purchased a children's Storybook Bible weeks before because ours was falling apart. I bought an extra one which I was planning to give away on Instagram at the beginning of December because we love their Advent plan. Advent had already started and the bible was still sitting on my desk. I never found the time or energy to do the giveaway.

I saw it lying on my desk one morning, and I prayed quickly, "Lord, show me who to give this to." Instantly, He layed someone on my heart. But it wasn't a friend, or acquaintance, or even a friend from Instagram…it was a complete stranger. My heart pounded a little, and I thought, "No, no, that's crazy," and I tried to brush the feeling aside or write it off as my idea and not His.

You see the night before I had sold some old book shelves on Facebook. A woman that I didn't know came and picked them up. Then the next morning, I had posted another kid's toy that I was selling, and she messaged me that she would like that too. God was asking me to give her this Bible.

This is not something I do. Really, I had never done anything like this. Not with a stranger. I even told myself, I don't do things like this. I think we can so easily tell ourselves that it takes someone extra bold or gifted to tell about Jesus to complete strangers, when really God asks this of all of us. When we see people spread Jesus in an evangelistic way, we are simply watching someone with a willing and obedient heart.

All day long, I couldn't shake this thought. As the day progressed, inching towards the time that she would come to pick up the toy, I became more and more nervous.

A friend messaged me, telling me that she was going to do the advent devotional with her kids, but didn't have the Bible. I began writing that I had an extra one for her that I could give her, but before I sent it, I slowly deleted the entire message. I was so close to missing what God had for me.

Time slowly inched towards dinner time. She would be at my house any minute. I was sweating as I cooked for my family with one eye out the window watching our driveway. I was terrified to give it to her, but I was becoming more afraid that I would choose not to. I grabbed the Bible, and wrote in the front of it, "God loves you so much! I pray that you see His love for you," and I went back to the kitchen. There was no turning back now.

As I saw her pull in, I was a mess, but I knew God had put this woman in my life two times within 24 hours for a reason. I walked outside, Bible in hand. She stepped out of her truck, and this time pulled out a three year old girl. The instant I looked into the little girl's eyes, I instantly knew this bible was for her. A calming peace swept over me. I knew God wanted this for her, and amazingly, He was using me to be a part of it.

I walked over to the woman and said, "I don't know why, but God has been asking me all day to give this to you." I handed it to her, and she instantly started weeping…in my driveway, simply picking up her Facebook purchase. I put my arm around her and asked her if I could pray for her. She said yes and told me that she had been having a really hard time. She briefly described some of her struggles, and as I pulled her close, I prayed.

I walked away from those few minutes of obedience in awe of how God could use me if I simply listened and obeyed. I would have been satisfied with the outcome of simply this, but the next morning God began to show off and build my trust in His voice and His workings. The woman messaged me on Facebook, telling me that she had been praying for God to show up in her life. She had recently left an abusive relationship, and she was desperate for her drug addicted adult son to willingly move out of her house because she could no longer live there with him. That morning, her son had texted her that he was moving out and that she could move back into her house. She told me that because of what I did, she knew that God was saying, I see you, I love you, and keep going.

I don't want us focusing on what I did, but rather what God did. Through my obedience, and really not many words, He clearly spoke to this woman's heart and showed her that He is with her.

Let's step back a few verses. Let's read **Ezekiel 37:4-6.**
   "He said to me, 'Prophesy concerning these bones and say to them: Dry bones, hear the word of the LORD! This is what the Lord God says to these bones: I will cause breath to enter you, and you will live. I will put tendons on you, make flesh grow on you, and cover you with skin. I will put breath in you so that you come to life. Then you will know that I am the LORD."

God told Ezekiel exactly what to say to the bones and says that **then he will know that He is the Lord.**

When we are obedient to what God asks of us, our eyes open up to see more of Him! He comes into focus! He becomes bigger! We get to see more of His power, His love, and His holiness. When we see Him work through our obedience, we are more in awe of Him than ever before, and we know that, truly, **HE IS THE LORD!**

So, what is He asking of you?

Often when we ask this of ourselves, we direct it towards the question, "What is God's calling on my life?" Or we ask God questions about what we are meant to do in life, the big dreams that may be years away. Let us not get distracted by this. It is in the daily obedience that these bigger callings grow from. If we cannot be obedient in the small, daily ways, how are we going to be obedient in the big ways? It takes tiny steps of obedience to grow our confidence in knowing His voice and trusting that His ways are so much better than our ways.

In my healing journey of three years, there were hundreds, if not thousands, of tiny steps of obedience along the way. Some I can see as bigger, such as calling for my first counseling session, signing up for Revelation Wellness Instructor training, or writing and sharing my testimony. But there were many more times of small obediences like choosing not to numb out when the emotional pain was tearing me apart, reading my Bible when I would rather not, going on prayer walks when I wanted to stay with my kids and distract myself instead, eating the vegetable instead of comforting myself with sugar, revisiting the pain often in between counseling sessions instead of ignoring it, and journaling out the hurt as God revealed more and more of the depth of it.

We want to believe that these are the small things, when really, they are the BIG things. This is where the transformation happens. This is where we come alive! This is where we get to see how big our God is, and yet, at the same time, how intentional and loving He is in the ways that He cares for us.

This week, I want you to continually be asking God what your next step of obedience is. Maybe you will even be bold enough to pray the "anything" prayer and tell God that you will do ANYTHING that He asks of you.

What is He asking you to do? Or not do. This may be a big thing, but it also may be in tiny little obediences throughout your day. Don't just ask Him though…when you have an inkling of the answer, **go and do it! Show up and I promise, He will show up!**

Homework : Week 6

Many times obedience requires sacrifice. A temple is ready for worship after a sacrifice has been made. In 2 Chronicles 29, King Hezekiah is restoring worship and bringing it back to the Lord's temple.

2 Chronicles 29:15-19 says,
"They gathered their brothers together, consecrated themselves, and went according to the king's command by the words of the Lord to cleanse the Lord's temple.

The priests went to the entrance of the Lord's temple to cleanse it. They took all the unclean things they found in the Lord's sanctuary to the courtyard of the Lord's temple. Then the Levites received them and took them outside to the Kidron Valley. They began the consecration on the first day of the first month, and on the eighth day of the month they came to the portico of the Lord's temple. They consecrated the Lord's temple for eight days, and on the sixteenth day of the first month they finished.

Then they went inside to King Hezekiah and said, 'We have cleansed the whole temple of the Lord, the altar of burnt offering and all its utensils, and the table for the rows of the Bread of the Presence and all its utensils. We have set up and consecrated all the utensils that King Ahaz rejected during his reign when he became unfaithful. They are in front of the altar of the Lord.'"

Then we read in 2 Chronicles 29:27-30,
"Then Hezekiah ordered that the burnt offering be offered on the altar. When the burnt offerings began, the song of the Lord and the trumpets began, accompanied by the instruments of King David of Israel. The whole assembly was worshiping, singing the song, and blowing the trumpets —all this continued until the burnt offering was completed. When the burnt offerings were completed, the king and all those present with him bowed down and worshiped. Then King Hezekiah and the officials told the Levites to sing praise to the Lord in the words of David and of the seer Asaph. So they sang praises with rejoicing and knelt low and worshiped."

Why are we looking at this? Because our bodies are now the temple of God. No longer do we have to sacrifice animals in our place to cleanse ourselves from sin, Jesus came and did that once and for all. But to bring our bodies and our whole selves to a place of pure worship, it often begins with the cleansing of sacrifice.

Romans 12:1 says,
"Therefore, brothers and sisters, in view of the mercies of God, I urge you to present your bodies as a living sacrifice, holy and pleasing to God; this is your true worship."

Sacrifice begins our worship, and **IT IS OUR WORSHIP**.

1. **What may God be asking you to sacrifice out of obedience and worship right now? Is it possible He is calling you to a fast of some kind?**

   a. Adele Ahlberg Calhoun describes a fast as, "the self-denial of normal necessities in order to intentionally attend to God in prayer. Bringing attachments and cravings to the surface opens a place for prayer. The physical awareness of emptiness is the reminder to turn to Jesus who alone can satisfy."

   She also says, "Fasting is an opportunity to lay down an appetite - an appetite for food, for media, for shopping. This act of self-denial may not seem huge - it's just a meal or a trip to the mall - but it brings us face to face with the hunger at the core of our being. Fasting exposes how we try to keep empty hunger at bay and gain a sense of well-being by devouring creature comforts. Through self-denial we begin to recognize what controls us. Our small denials of the self show us just how little taste we actually have for sacrifice or time with God."[1]

   b. Fasting often reveals what we are craving more than God. It is a way to cleanse our temple of those things just as we read in 2 Chronicles.

   c. There are so many things you can fast from. Whether God is calling you to fast from social media, shopping, tv, or actual food, it should not be something that is easy for you to do. It should be something that brings you closer to Jesus because you can only do it with His strength. As you fast, every time you crave the thing you are fasting from, turn to God's word or prayer. Replace your craving with a craving for time with God.

2. **What sin do you need to confess?**

   a. Often, we know our sin, yet we do not go through the act of confessing it to God. It can feel scary or shame inducing, but what we are doing is opening ourselves up within the safety of a divine love. Our hearts are seeking transformation. We are coming to our Father desiring growth. We are moving towards looking more and more like Jesus.

   b. Sometimes, we don't see our sin. This is when we need to pray...

   Psalm 139:23-24.
   "Search me, God, know my heart;
   test me and know my concerns.
   See if there is any offensive way in me;
   lead me in the everlasting way."

   c. Begin to confess your sin to God this week. Confess your weaknesses. Ask Him to reveal the areas of sin that you do not see. This will set you FREE!

3. **Are you holding onto some unforgiveness?**

    a. Colossians 3:12-13 says, "Therefore, as God's chosen people, holy and dearly loved, clothe yourselves with compassion, kindness, humility, gentleness and patience. Bear with each other and forgive one another if any of you has a grievance against someone. Forgive as the Lord forgave you." (NIV)

    b. "The lie the enemy tells us about forgiveness is that if we forgive, we are saying that what was done to us (or said about us) was okay, that it was not wrong, that it was 'no big deal.' Forgiveness is not about excusing the actions of others; it is about removing the impact of those actions from our lives. When Jesus forgave us on the cross, He was not saying that sin was 'no big deal,' He was removing sin's ability to continue to separate us from our Heavenly Father and all of His Kingdom. Unforgiveness isolates us. It cuts us off. It keeps us from being who we were created - in love, by love, and for love - to be. But forgiveness, glorious Christlike forgiveness, plugs us into the heart of the Father, all that He is, and all that He has." (Robert Hotchkin)[2]

"I know forgiveness can be excruciatingly hard. It can seem like one of the most unfair of all God's commands. But we must remember who is asking us to forgive. God. He is the Father of compassion and God of all comfort. So, as we navigate forgiveness within the complexities of relationships where we've been deeply wounded and sometimes even abused, God's command to forgive is not absent of His compassion and comfort." (Lysa TerKeurst)[3]

Forgiveness for betrayal, abuse, and deep hurts is beyond difficult. We are not going to make light of this or act like this can happen overnight, but we also are not going to pretend that God does not want us to forgive. Forgiveness isn't just a part of Christianity, it is Christianity. It is what Jesus died for, and it is what He calls us to do. Not simply because it is what we are supposed to do, but because He knows that it is what is best for us and that it will bring us to FREEDOM!

    c. Forgiveness releases a weight from your life. This week, talk to God about where you may need to forgive. Be honest with Him about where you have been hurt, and why it may be hard for you to forgive. Journal your thoughts and keep handing this over to God.
If you are struggling in the area of Forgiveness, I highly recommend reading Forgiving What You Can't Forget by Lysa TerKeurst.

4. Take time to worship God!

a. Through your sacrifice, forgiveness and confession, God is going to work in and through you. Worship Him for what He has done! Worship Him remembering what He has done in you and around you in your past. Worship Him for what He is going to do in the future because of His promises!

b. Take time every day this week to play a song that you can close your eyes, move your body in dance, lift your arms up and worship God. Pick a song of your choice or go and listen to "Yes I will" by Vertical Worship or "Jubilee" by Maverick City Music.

Begin to Be Restored in Stages

"As I looked, tendons appeared on them, flesh grew, and skin covered them, but there was no breath in them. He said to me, "Prophesy to the breath, prophesy, son of man. Say to it: This is what the Lord God says: Breath, come from the four winds and breathe into these slain so that they may live!" So I prophesied as he commanded me; the breath entered them, and they came to life and stood on their feet, a vast army."
Ezekiel 37:8-10

You did it! I am so very proud of you for pouring yourself into every week these past six weeks! Let's review the stages of coming alive that we have learned.

- We must first recognize that there was once life in us.
- We then need to trust that God will breathe life back into us.
- We have to choose to step up and take action.
- We need to use the power of God's Word and Truth over our lives.
- We allow the Holy Spirit to breathe into us.
- We must obey what He is asking us to do.

Then what? We come to life like never before and walk free the rest of our lives? That's not quite how it works.

Let's read Ezekiel 37:8-10.
"As I looked, tendons appeared on them, flesh grew, and skin covered them, but there was no breath in them. He said to me, 'Prophesy to the breath, prophesy, son of man. Say to it: This is what the Lord God says: Breath, come from the four winds and breathe into these slain so that they may live!' So I prophesied as he commanded me; the breath entered them, and they came to life and stood on their feet, a vast army."

The bones didn't come back to life all at once. **The bones were restored back to life in stages.** First the tendons appeared, then flesh grew, then the skin covered them, yet they still were not alive. Then God asked Ezekiel to say more, to prophesy to the breath. Again, he did as God commanded, and they came to life.

These steps that we have walked through these past few weeks are just the beginning. You will be restored in stages. Like we have said from the very beginning, the deep transformation of coming back to life can only be done by the Holy Spirit in God's timing. We must do the work like we have talked about, yet leave the outcome up to God.

As Ezekiel called on the breath to come and breathe life back into the bodies, we must also call on the Holy Spirit to do the work in us that only He can do. He is the only one who can fully free you! He is the only one that will bring you back to life!

This process that we have gone through is not a direct line with a start and a finish. It is more like a circle. This is a process that we will continue over and over again. It is a process that we have to choose to actively pursue throughout our life, each time growing closer and closer to our Father. Trusting Him, obeying Him, inviting Him, and being blown away by what He can do when we open ourselves up to His working.

Come Alive Now

recognize
THERE WAS ONCE LIFE IN YOU

trust
GOD AND HIS LOVE FOR YOU

stand up
TAKE ACTION

hear
THE WORD OF THE LORD

breathe
ALLOW THE HOLY SPIRIT TO
BREATHE INTO YOU

obey
SACRIFICE, OBEDIENCE, AND
WORSHIP BRINGS FREEDOM

CREATED BY LEAH FRUTH

I encourage you to keep this circle active in your life. There will be tough times ahead. Days that we slide back. Days that we feel like we are in a weird funk. Days that we feel as if we need to climb out of a deep hole. Let us prepare now for those days.

The very last homework that I am going to give you is to create a battle plan. What is your battle plan for the days that you cannot muster up the energy to attempt any part of the circle of action steps? How are you going to begin to climb out of the hole?

Create a battle plan of 5 steps.

Here is my battle plan to use as an example but I encourage you to create your own.

1. Drink an entire glass of water.
2. Turn on my worship playlist. Loud!
   Last year, I used one song over and over again called "Way Maker" by Leeland.
3. Move my body in some way.
   Sometimes that is dancing to the song, sometimes it is walking slowly, sometimes it is a dead sprint on my treadmill.
4. Pray.
   Sometimes this is slow breath prayers, sometimes desperate sobbing prayers, sometimes it is stating the promises of God that I need to see Him working in.
5. Thank Him!
   Gratefulness turns my eyes to what He is doing and has already done in my life. It turns my eyes to the good. It reminds me of His faithfulness.

Remember this is a war. Do not let up. Use these verses from Ephesians to guide you in creating your battle plan.

Ephesians 6:10-18 says,
" Finally, be strengthened by the Lord and by his vast strength. Put on the full armor of God so that you can stand against the schemes of the devil. For our struggle is not against flesh and blood, but against the rulers, against the authorities, against the cosmic powers of this darkness, against evil, spiritual forces in the heavens. For this reason take up the full armor of God, so that you may be able to resist in the evil day, and having prepared everything, to take your stand. Stand, therefore, with truth like a belt around your waist, righteousness like armor on your chest, and your feet sandaled with readiness for the gospel of peace. In every situation take up the shield of faith with which you can extinguish all the flaming arrows of the evil one. Take the helmet of salvation and the sword of the Spirit—which is the word of God. Pray at all times in the Spirit with every prayer and request, and stay alert with all perseverance and intercession for all the saints."

With God by your side and with God as your focus, you can do this!

I am so incredibly grateful for you trusting me to guide you through this time! Thank you from the bottom of my heart.

This is my final prayer for you.
"I pray that he may grant you, according to the riches of his glory, to be strengthened with power in your inner being through his Spirit, and that Christ may dwell in your hearts through faith. I pray that you, being rooted and firmly established in love, may be able to comprehend with all the saints what is the length and width, height and depth of God's love, and to know Christ's love that surpasses knowledge, so that you may be filled with all the fullness of God. Now to him who is able to do above and beyond all that we ask or think according to the power that works in us— to him be glory in the church and in Christ Jesus to all generations, forever and ever. Amen."
Ephesians 3:16-21

It is time. Come alive now!

Praying for you friend,
Leah

My Battle Plan

When I'm in a funk, anxiety is high, or I just can't shake it
I will...

01

02

03

04

05

Notes

Notes

Notes

Acknowledgments

God: He sure knows how thankful I am, but I will tell him over and over again. God, you made me a writer, yet it took me a long time to know that you made me to write about you. I can't believe that you chose me to do this, but I am grateful every day. You set me free and brought so much joy and peace to my life that I could have never dreamt possible, and now I will never stop telling people about how good you are.

Trevor: You have always been my biggest supporter and cheerleader. I don't know if there is anything you don't believe I can do and that alone gives me such confidence to go after whatever God is calling me to. I love the life that we have built together.

My kids, Jasper, Ellis and Crosby: You are my reason for all of this. You gave me the desire to seek God because I wanted you to seek God. You asked questions about God that I didn't know so I had to dig in and learn. You deserved a mom that was present and healed and so I sought after healing. It's all because of you. Thank you for always cheering me on, coming alongside me In ministry, and being more excited about this book really happening than anyone else.

Janessa, Sara, Courtney, and Delaney: The gratitude for your friendship and your support could never be fully expressed. Thank you for never shying away from real struggles and real life. Thank you for being my safe place. Your prayers have held me up.

Lauren: You have let me into your story, and so often I am writing for you. You are a friend and the greatest encourager. I believe in myself so often because you believe in me.

Angela: You grabbed ahold of me, quite literally, and I have not been the same since. I am so glad that God put you in my life. You have shown me a God that is loving and powerful. One that still heals and does miracles right in front of our eyes. Thank you for all of this and so much more. Thank you for being my help and partner in this book publishing process.

Tabitha, Jennifer, April, Lindsey, Sarah, and Kaylie: You welcomed me into your writing group when I desperately needed to believe that I was a writer. You made the dream feel real and achievable. And how could I ever thank you enough for being my community in the long year of 2020. You will all forever hold a very special place in my heart.

Sherri: God knew I needed you. He knew I needed to be healed from my pain and grief before I could ever begin to write for others. Thank you for doing your job so well and so softly. This book would have never been written without your counseling.

Alisa Keeton and Revelation Wellness: You changed me! You were instrumental in healing my mind and body and helped bring me into who I was always created to be. I don't know where I would be without your ministry. Thank you for being faithful to the call.

Geoff and Jill: There are no words other than I love you two so much. You have been such caring, loving, and sweet guidance in my life. The joy and pride I see in your eyes when you look at me is a side of God that I have needed to see here on Earth. Jesus in you makes me want to know Jesus more.

My Church Family and Leaders: Thank you for always supporting me. You gave me a way to use my gifts the instant I fell in love with Jesus, and you have allowed me to use my voice first. The prayers and encouragement I get from you can never be fully counted. You all are my family.

Linda: Thank you for your encouragement. Thank you for reading and editing these words. I am so grateful.

Endnotes

Week 1:

1. Keller, Timothy. 2014. Every Good Endeavor: Connecting Your Work to God's Work. N.p.: Penguin Publishing Group.
2. "Alisa Keeton - Today, God woke me with these words. ...." 2020. Facebook. https://www.facebook.com/akeeton/posts/today-god-woke-me-with-these-wordsyou-know-i-love-the-quote-from-tim-keller-abou/2522654981173970/.

Week 2:

1. Rubio, Nicole, dir. 2020. Grey's Anatomy. Season 16, episode 12, "The Last Supper."
2. Myers, Raechel, Amanda B. Williams, and CSB Bibles by Holman. 2017. CSB She Reads Truth Bible, Hardcover. Edited by Raechel Myers and Amanda B. Williams. N.p.: B&H Publishing Group.
3. "Prayers on Surrender." n.d. Prayer Room. Accessed January 22, 2024. https://prayer.knowing-jesus.com/Prayers-on-Surrender.

Week 3:

1. McDaniel, Debbie. 2015. "40 Inspiring Quotes from Elisabeth Elliot." Crosswalk. https://www.crosswalk.com/faith/spiritual-life/inspiring-quotes/40-inspiring-quotes-from-elisabeth-elliot.html.
2. Barton, Ruth H. 2011. Sacred Rhythms: Spiritual Practices That Nourish Your Soul and Transform Your Life. N.p.: Zondervan.
3. "Revelation Wellness." n.d. Revelation Wellness: https://www.revelationwellness.org.

Week 4:

1. Cherry, Kendra, Brian Tracy, and MARISA PEER. 2019. "The Differences Between Your Conscious and Subconscious Mind." Marisa Peer. https://marisapeer.com/the-differences-between-your-conscious-and-subconscious-mind/.
2. Leaf, Caroline, and Leaf. 2015. Switch On Your Brain: The Key to Peak Happiness, Thinking, and Health. N.p.: Baker Publishing Group.
3. Allen, Jennie. 2020. Get Out of Your Head: Stopping the Spiral of Toxic Thoughts. N.p.: Crown Publishing Group.
4. "Blue Letter Bible." n.d. Blue Letter Bible: Bible Search and Study Tools. https://www.blueletterbible.org.
5. "The Bible Project." n.d. Study the Story of the Bible With Free Tools. https://bibleproject.com.

Week 5:

1. "Benefits of Deep Breathing." n.d. Urban Balance. Accessed January 10, 2024. https://www.urbanbalance.com/benefits-deep-breathing/.
2. Calhoun, Adele A. 2015. Spiritual Disciplines Handbook: Practices That Transform Us. N.p.: InterVarsity Press.
3. Joshua 4:1-9
4. See Calhoun, Adele A.

Week 6:

1. See Calhoun, Adele A.
2. Hotchkin, Robert. 2016. Leviathan Exposed: Overcoming the Hidden Schemes of a Demonic King. N.p.: XP Publishing.
3. TerKeurst, Lysa. 2020. Forgiving What You Can't Forget: Discover How to Move On, Make Peace with Painful Memories, and Create a Life That's Beautiful Again. N.p.: Nelson Books.

Stay in Touch

I am beyond grateful for our time together. There is nothing better than learning to love God more alongside my fellow sisters in Christ.

Please keep in touch! You can do that by going to my website, www.leahfruth.com. While you're there, sign up for my email newsletter so that we can stay close, or follow me on Instagram or Facebook (@leahfruth).

I would love to hear from you, too! Share your story from this journey of coming alive with me by contacting me through my website.

With much love,
Leah